Contents

What is a chicken?

A chicken is a bird. All birds have
feathers, a beak and a pair of wings.
A female chicken is called a **hen** and a
male chicken is called a **cockerel**. Baby
chickens are called **chicks**. All chickens
begin life in an egg.

comb

adult hen

beak

wing

How an egg grows into a chicken

Written by
Rita Kant

Illustrated by
Carolyn Franklin

Crack!

Hold the page
up to the light
to see the chick
inside the egg.

BOOK HOUSE

Published in Great Britain in 2009 by
Book House, an imprint of
The Salariya Book Company Ltd
25 Marlborough Place, Brighton BN1 1UB

SALARIYA

HB ISBN 978-1-906370-38-1
PB ISBN 978-1-906370-39-8

Visit our website at **www.book-house.co.uk**
or go to **www.salariya.com** for free electronic versions of:
You Wouldn't Want to be an Egyptian Mummy!
You Wouldn't Want to be a Roman Gladiator!
Avoid Joining Shackleton's Polar Expedition!
Avoid Sailing on a 19th-Century Whaling Ship!

Author: **Tanya Kant** is a graduate of the University of
Sussex at Brighton, England. She specialises in writing and
editing children's non-fiction, and is especially interested in
natural science and history. She lives in Hove, England.

Artist: **Carolyn Franklin** graduated from Brighton
College of Art with a focus on design and illustration. Since
then she has worked in animation, advertising, and children's
fiction and non-fiction. She has a special interest in natural
history and has written many books on the subject, including
Life in the Wetlands in the WHAT ON EARTH? series and *Egg
to Owl* in the CYCLES OF LIFE series.

Consultant: **Monica Hughes** is an experienced
educational advisor and author of more than one hundred
books for young children. She has been head teacher of a
primary school, primary advisory teacher, and senior lecturer
in early childhood education.

Editor: **Stephen Haynes**

A catalogue record for this book is available
from the British Library.
Printed in China.

comb

beak

wattle

adult cockerel

wing

Why do hens build nests?

All hens lay eggs. Before a hen lays her eggs, she builds a soft, warm **nest** to keep them safe. She uses straw to make the nest, and lines it with her own soft feathers.

hen gathering straw to make a nest

straw

Once the nest is built, the hen can lay
her eggs. She lays one or two eggs a
day until she has about twelve.

What *is* inside an egg?

A hen's eggs are **fertilised** when the hen and cockerel **mate**. An egg will **hatch** into a chicken only if it has been fertilised. Each fertilised egg holds and protects something that will grow into a baby bird.

The eggs that we eat are not fertilised. They do not have a baby bird inside.

eggs

How does the chick grow inside the egg?

At first the young chick inside the egg is just a tiny dot called an **embryo**. As the embryo grows, it slowly begins to look like a bird.

The egg also contains yellow **yolk**. The baby chick feeds on the yolk, which helps it to grow.

The embryo and yolk lie in egg white or **albumen**. This jelly-like substance protects the embryo and helps it grow.

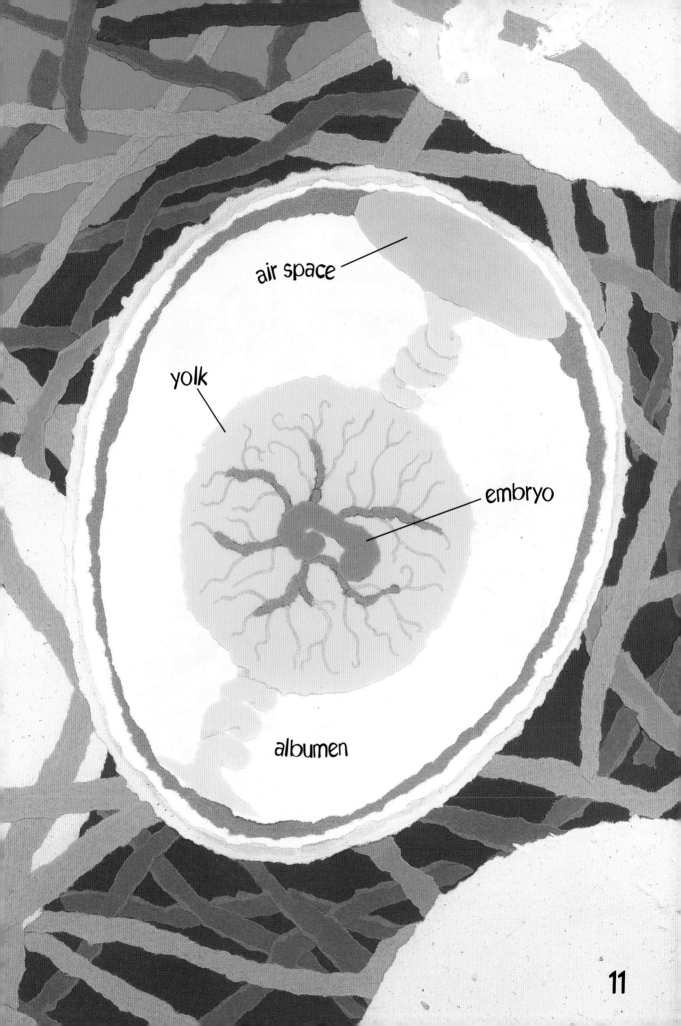

air space

yolk

embryo

albumen

Why does a hen sit on her eggs?

A hen sits on her eggs to keep them warm. This is called **brooding**. The eggs don't break because their shells are strong and hard.

soft feathers

The mother hen surrounds the eggs with her soft feathers. Every now and then she turns the eggs to keep them warm all over.

cluck
cluck

The hen calls to her chicks.

When does the egg hatch?

After 21 days, the baby chick inside the egg starts to make a cheeping noise. This lets the hen know that her chicks are about to hatch. The hen makes a clucking sound to encourage them to come out. All of the eggs will hatch at around the same time.

Hold this page up to the light to see the chicks hatch.

Soon the eggshells begin to crack.

Crack!

Cheep cheep

15

egg tooth

wet chick

How does the chick break free from its egg?

The chick has a little point on its beak which is called an **egg tooth.** It uses this to make a hole in the eggshell from the inside. It takes a few hours for the chick to break free. When it first hatches, the chick is wet and slimy all over. The chick soon dries out and looks like a fluffy, round ball.

Cheep cheep cheep

What do chicks eat?

Even very young chicks eat the same foods as their mother. They **peck** and scratch at the ground, looking for grains, seeds and grubs. The chicks make cheeping sounds all the time so their mother knows where they are.

hen

Cheep
cheep

seed

Chicks peck and wander.

At first the chicks follow
their mother. As they get
older, they start to explore
their new surroundings.

The fluffy chick grows.

grub

grain

When does a chick start to look like a chicken?

As the chick gets older, new feathers start to grow. In a few months, the chick will lose its fluffy yellow feathers and grow silky brown adult ones. A young hen is ready to lay her first eggs when she is about 25 weeks old.

worm

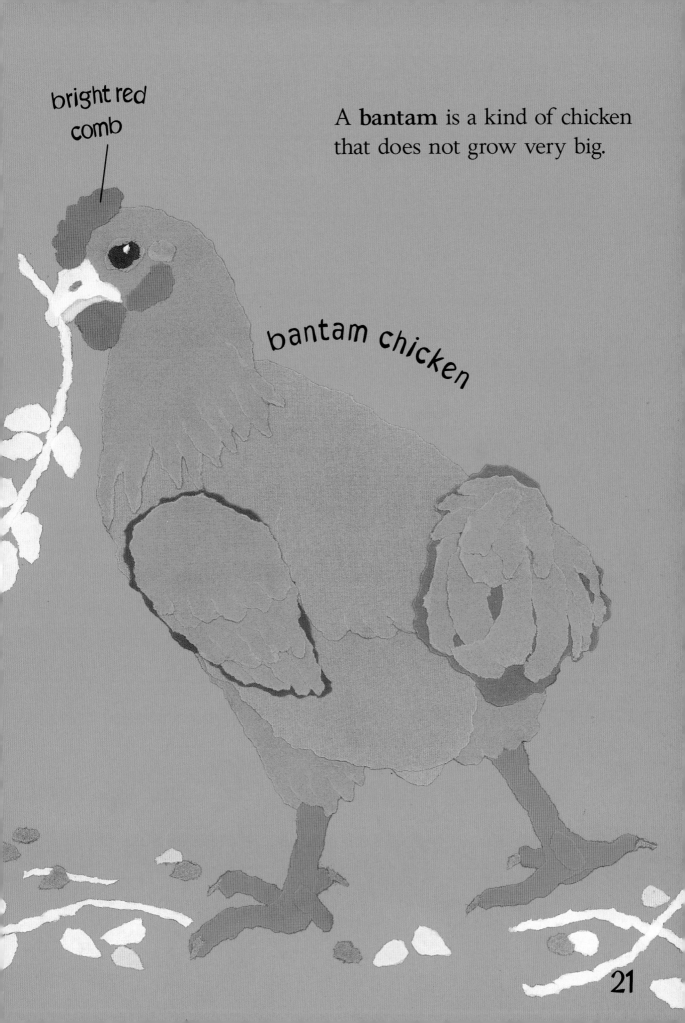

bright red
comb

A **bantam** is a kind of chicken
that does not grow very big.

bantam chicken

What animals like to eat chicken eggs?

Birds, foxes, lizards and snakes all like to eat eggs. To get at the food inside, some animals bite or peck at the eggshell. Others smash it with stones. Snakes like to swallow eggs whole!

squawk!

hungry fox

hen protecting
her eggs

The hen tries to
protect her eggs.
She flaps her wings
and makes noises to
scare the fox away.

Why do humans keep chickens?

Humans keep chickens for their eggs and meat. They are often kept on farms, in barns, or in specially built shelters called **coops**.

Cheep cheep

A group of chickens is called a **flock**. Flocks are usually made up of just hens and their chicks. Sometimes a flock has a cockerel, too.

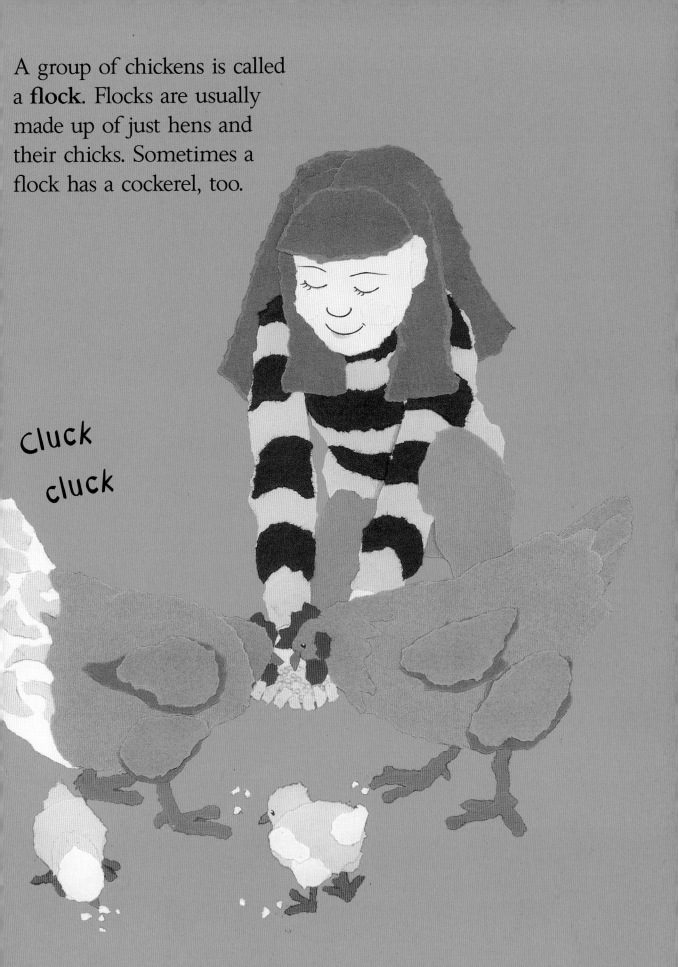

Cluck

cluck

Chicken facts

Wild chickens live in the tropical forests of Asia, Africa and South America. They are called jungle fowl.

A good laying hen will lay 250 to 300 eggs a year.

Young hens often lay eggs that have two yolks.

Eggs are stronger than you think. A typical chicken egg will support a weight of nearly 5 kilograms before breaking.

An average chicken weighing 2.5 kilograms has a wingspan of around 85 centimetres.

A frizzle is a type of chicken
with curly feathers. Silkies
have very soft, fluffy
feathers.

The White Sully is said to be
the biggest and heaviest breed
of chicken. The Serama
bantam from South-East Asia
is said to be the smallest.

Cluck cluck

Cheep cheep

27

Things to do

Ask an adult to help you with these experiments!

How strong is an egg?

Do this experiment over a sink, just in case you make a mistake. Place an egg in the palm of your hand. Close your hand so that your fingers are completely wrapped around the egg. Squeeze the egg by applying even pressure all around the shell.

If you do it correctly, the egg will not break. This is because the pressure from your fingers is spread all over the surface of the egg.

It's easy to crack an egg on the side of a bowl, because the pressure is all on one side of the egg.

The floating egg

1. Put a raw egg in a cup of water. Does the egg float or sink?

2. It should sink — unless it's old. (Older eggs have pockets of air in them.)

3. Add 8 tablespoons of salt to the water and stir. What happens now?

4. Stirring makes the salt dissolve into the water. The added salt makes the water more dense than the egg. The egg will now float above the denser salt water.

Life cycle of a chicken

2 days

13 days

adult hen

20 days

one day old

just hatched

Words to remember

Albumen The clear, jelly-like substance inside an egg that protects the embryo and the yolk. It is also called egg white.

Bantam A small type of chicken.

Brood To sit on eggs to keep them warm.

Chick A baby chicken.

Cockerel An adult male chicken.

Coop A shelter for chickens.

Egg tooth A little point on the tip of a chick's beak that helps it to break the shell of its egg.

Embryo The first stage in the growth of the chicken inside the egg.

Fertilised egg An egg laid by a hen which has mated with a cockerel. A chick can grow only in a fertilised egg.

Flock A group of chickens.

Hatch To break out of an egg.

Hen An adult female chicken.

Mate To join together to make a baby animal.

Nest A safe place made by the hen for laying her eggs.

Peck To jab at or bite with the beak.

Wattle A loose piece of skin that hangs from the neck of an adult chicken.

Yolk The yellow substance inside an egg that feeds the embryo.

Index